MW01017033

Cult Life

Kyeren Regehr

Cult Life

Kyeren Regehr

PEDLAR PRESS | ST. JOHN'S

Copyright © Kyeren Regehr 2020

Pedlar Press supports copyright. Copyright fuels creativity, encourages diverse voices, promotes free speech, and creates a vibrant culture. Thank you for buying an authorized edition of this book and for complying with copyright laws by not reproducing, scanning, or distributing any part of it in any form without permission. You are supporting writers and allowing Pedlar to continue to publish books for every reader.

All Rights Reserved

For information, write Pedlar Press at
113 Bond Street, St. John's NL A1C 1T6 Canada

Cover Art   Emily Critch, *Chairs*, photopolymer, 9.5" x 12", 2017
Design   Emma Dawn Allain
Typeface   Avenir / Baskerville
Printed in Canada Coach House Printing, Toronto

Library and Archives Canada Cataloguing in Publication

Title: Cult life / Kyeren Regehr.

Names: Regehr, Kyeren, 1971- author.

Description: Poems.

Identifiers: Canadiana 20190196041 | ISBN 9781989424001 (softcover)

Classification: LCC PS8635.E3933 C85 2020 | DDC C811/.6—dc23

Acknowledgements

The publisher wishes to thank the Canada Council for the Arts and the NL Publishers Assistance Program for their generous support of our publishing program.

For Chris—
we've journeyed a long way
to find ourselves
in each other

CONTENTS

PART I

PART II

PART III

I

…Look at all those women wearing deep blue saris, leaning
this way and that, in the ocean. Thousands, row on row. Are they
moaning or praying?…

—Anne Simpson

Inventory

Poets treat their experiences shamelessly: they exploit them.
                        —Friedrich Neitzsche

Nine Vipassana meditators stuck
in the cycle of craving. Five ex-Krishnas,
six Transcendentals, four Sai Baba devotees—
one raped by a dhobi at the Puttaparti ashram.
A pair of Ashtanga yoga instructors flipping headstands
in back of the dining hall. A visiting Tibetan Buddhist,
two Scientologists, seventeen grazing seekers
hugged by Amma. One spooky Rosicrucian,
one moony Wiccan priestess, eight Osho followers
pretzeled in tantric rapture, a Brazilian trance-healer
channelling the famous Dr.Fritz, performing
psychic surgery on the faithful.
Three loudmouths quoting Da Free John,
a rather fragrant incense maker
from Sri Aurobindo's, one wondering sadhu,
                        wandering on.

One lab assistant to a quantum physicist
turned New Age pyramid marketer, peddling magical water.
One chiropractor, two Reiki masters, a homeopathic
kinesiologist, a palmful of oily massage therapists
in and out of bedrooms, uncricking necks,
jumpstarting meridians. Three chartered accountants
diddling the books, and a high-end psychic once hired to sense
glitches in corporate power. One Mary Kay millionaire,
two trust fund babies—all hoovered clean
                        long before they leave.

One florid French painter hanging art
in the foyer, waiting for The Master
to declare his wizardry. A brawny Austrian
philosopher renaming himself Vinnie, eleven Aussies,
mostly bronzed, expected to perform words like *G'day*.
One iffy guy with a black-toothed grin
hiding out in a basement room,
                    rumoured to have been a pedophile.

Seven twenty-somethings singing passionately in Polish,
dunking each other in the pool. Eight cool Kiwis,
two hot Russians, half a pint of warm Brits,
four Dutch waiters over six-foot-three. A clutch of Canadians
hunting green cards—one woos an ex-stripper
with a pawnshop glitterbit,
                    ditches her a week post-vows.

Four sous chefs, six line cooks,
thirteen hopeful waitresses. Half a dozen handymen
quietly hammering, screwing towel hooks, hanging
mirrors in the bathrooms of the waitresses.
A twelve-pack of pre-teens, a skewed diamond
of little leaguers, one gifted kid in a wheelchair,
five barefoot toddlers with mucky faces,
and an eight-year-old sociopath pied-pipering
the littlies over the highway
                    and deep into the cornfields.

Six single moms, two jilted dads,
two trenchant lesbian couples, candying the kids,
cold-shouldering the parents. Three women with cancer

careening around The Master, expecting
to be healed—they all pass,
three, two, one, through dorm room 203.
One man on the quiet borrowing lacy
lingerie from the laundry room. Norma-Jean's
soul twin with an urgent smile,
tangled in a sheet, exposing
                        a nipple at her window.

One two-timing double bass jazz genius,
one real Broadway dancer from *Cats*,
one concert pianist with arthritic perfect pitch.
One opera baritone, his soprano spurned in Berlin.
One gay DJ wearing headphones like a tiara,
one emo prima ballerina who goes
Jim Morrison in a hotel bathtub
                        a month after leaving.

Seven lead guitarists, four half-decent
drummers, a full gospel choir, enough brass
for Motown. Two dozen amateur thespians
monologuing to save the world. A dresser
from London's West End ready to
                        rip the stitches out of physical existence.

A pathological narcissist who'll one day die
of self-awareness, a balding blues diva, an aging
would-be country queen, an ex-punk-rocker
who'd opened for D.O.A. in Regina. And a couple of writers—
the fiction gal now hob-nobbing Toronto's
writerly royalty, the poet handling histories
                        shamelessly.

Hector

(Giving *Satsang* at the sister ashram in Australia)

Look at her whooshing away back there. Flies in from Chicago, acts like she's been to Mecca. Watch out— she's kissed the wall! She's touched the feet of Christ! You're only ever trying to prove something to yourself. Why don't you trundle off to the beach?

Yeah, you. Grab your kid, go raise your arms in the air and jiggle your titties at the waves. You wanna visit the main ashram? Look inside your mind. This is mind projected outward. It's a dream for Chissakes—the sun, the sweet ocean breeze, Govinda's reclining cinema and that tender deep-fried cauliflower tempura, this carcass I'm *apparently* sitting in. It's all your mind. You want freedom? Want enlightenment? What's the thing which wants enlightenment? Think on this—

you get outta bed, middle of the night for a glass of water. Flip the kitchen light and a half dozen gargantuan Aussie cockroaches scuttle off real slow, like they're not too scared of you—those fucking big prehistoric things all armour plating and wings, and these segmented antenna, or is it antenni? Hell, I dunno. Point is, were they there *before* you flicked the switch? There's nothin going on here! If you don't take responsibility for everything in your mind you'll be reincarnating another thousand years—freedom is total responsibility. Did you hear me, guys?

You back there with the titties. Stop trying to prove you're awake and you might actually wake up. Whatever you're protecting—your kid, your precious identity— nothing here is real. You wanna shoot off to the land of snow? Then go. Twenty below right now. But hey, maybe that's the place in the space-time continuum where you finally ditch the dream. Don't fool yourself into thinking The Master's your ticket. Yeah, He'll shake your titties a bit, but you're not gonna find nothin there except your Self.

Spell of Dislocation

Summer of the twenty-eighth bedroom. I unpack
aura oils, fringed shawls, children's shoes, strata
of beach glass in jars, that film star photo of my father,

a worn copy of Neruda's *Yellow Heart*—"I beg you:
leave me restless. I live with the impossible ocean."
My mother always buttered the cats' paws,

watched them tongue off the old home's tang.
Bic to beeswax, I contain the four directions, cast
runestones along the sill, conjure a galah feather, ghost

gum leaf, smuggled through customs. My hand-whelped
quilt feral on this box spring—I'm sluiced dreaming
along Byron Bay's coastline, waves smashing

glassy on the lighthouse, mosaic brick of our beachside ashram
hippie-glinting like a magpie's nest, half the town
saronged and shoeless, other half blotto in the pubs.

Granddad's Old Holborn tobacco pouch ten hours south,
locked into my olfactory nerve like a homing beacon.
And I'm there, in his grease pit shed, machinery of the universe

stripped down on the benches. She's waiting too,
under the mulberry tree, juicy purpled bucket, spectacles
skew-whiff. One eye strangely green—a witch's door,

a hole in the hedge. *You won't be here too long,* she says.
I wake to pine needles sharpening the screen, my view:
o eucalypt with your rounded canopies, misty

blue air, dropping limbs in the sand, tossing
gum nuts like dice—where will we land?

Lorelei

Voila! The front desk, newbie! Messages hang out on this woven mat whatsit. On *Satsang* days Dear One will swoop down that staircase. Here, take a phone list. Ring Him *aaaany* time, like two AM. The Master's always available to us brothers, well, those fully committed, you gotta be able to handle whatever healing he hands you, this isn't easy street, sweetie. Folks zoom through like we've installed a spinny door.

So Shellie's your *official* guide, but Mojo Band's jamming—we have like five brother bands. You know Shellie is Dear One's daughter? What a groovy spirit guide you got! Visit her with tricky stuff, but *real* stuff, not *worldly* stuff, and don't wear out her light, 'kay? Reading room's here, lessons at eight. Sometimes He stays all *Satsang*, but it gets squeezy and kinda stinky cause the windows got painted shut last reno.

Wanna see the art room? Machines if you sew— we stitched nifty costumes for *Dreamcoat*. *Amaaaaazing* show, it was like out of time, baby! Audience was a bit scant though—*waaaay* too luminous for the humans. Some brothers silk-paint on those skinny tables, over there's glue and art hooey. I'm not a crafty gal, my fingers go goosey-loosey. Meet mister multi-purpose music room! For yoga, band rehearsals, choir too. Anyone can get sing-songy, except they do prefer you can sing, my ear's kinda tinny… I'm more a teacher of truth, and a fun'n'games gal.

Kitchen time, Sweetie! Service roster's that board, you're on it somewhere… You a baker? I'm buzzed on baking, made iced bagels for breakfast, sugar is totally transformational. (Take my advice girl, you're a tad bony for our boys.) Come to the *Satsang* room! Sit anywhere tomorrow, but hang backfield a bit so no bonnets ruffle. That's The Master's lazy chair and Blair's music cubby, he's our happy DJ, used to be a sad sack— we all get reborn, so say toodle-oo to yesterday's you. (It'll be a high-rise learning curve if you stay). Main laundry's down these stairs… so when you forget stuff after *Satsang*, and believe me you will, because the light here's fully powerful, not some itty-bitty pituitary stimulation, your whole head'll blow wide open, like you'll go *waaaaay* out, it'll knock your socks flying, baby—so treasures you forget Monday get stashed in Monday's box, and so on. At week's end they send it to The Barn, then it's a free-for-all—but mind the ghosties while you're grooving through the goodies. Found the cutest dotty dress—date night pour moi! Okay, what's left? Well, the relaxy-loungey library,

I dunno, you look like a reader.

Maisy's a fussy-gussy with her books, but take *aaaany* movies, jot your name in that hangy thingy. Top row's all The Master's videos, you *neeeeed* to watch these like last year, but you'll catch us up, maybe. The rest's *wordly* flics, but feel-good mystical. Here's a favey—*Phenomenon*. That Travolta's a sexy-cakes. Shame he's a Scientologist. So scout Shellie in *Satsang* in the AM—but Dorothy's the go-to-gal, from lost keys to bagging a bat in your room. Had one upside-downy from my curtain rod, f-reaky! Okie-dokie, *Jax* is chauffeuring me to Vespers. His light is so quasar. It's *lust-rous*. He opens my head like—*wooosh!*
You should totally come! If you wanna...
we can't drive you, but hang in the foyer around six-thirty, someone always swings newbies a ride.

Questing

To lose a long-haired surfer go somewhere
he'd never daydream his board. I mean,
who plans to run away *to* small town America?
Who flees a beachy barefoot paradise
to Nowhere Rednecksville with six suitcases,
a fold-up Fisher Price dollhouse

and a three-year-old child? I'm not really leaving,
I promise, indulge me another pilgrimage.
Like my half-baked trip to India, and the crystal healing
cacoethes, Kriya Yoga initiations,
Vipassana silences...
                           And my mother—

does she want to know ,
we've landed at a ramshackle resort the ashram owns?
That we're safer away from him?
In an unlocked building, ghosts and other
darknesses slugging the basement, sinking

cornerstones—will we ever find
home? At night I'm running
North with my daughter, through snow.
The sky glows white, everything's white;
maybe it's sand not snow, maybe it's Shangri-la
or a billowy formless Nirvana.

A Devotee's Daily Purification

Share a ride to five acres of pines, half-mowed fields,
sprawling sixties glass-front—the Healing Centre.
Deliver my child to Sunday Play, mandala drawing
with Marjeta; kid-brained labyrinths, M&M's cookies.

Potted geraniums in the atrium, lotus and closed eyes,
waiting for The Master. He often admires the flowers,
the perfection of their form in space-time, how they don't
long to be other than themselves; how pink geraniums
don't try to be red geraniums, or cowslips or daisies;

how His granddaughter gobbled a whole bloom of those
pungent velvety petals when she was two and wasn't that a hoot.
Each time he rolls that reel He's spooling us into His world,
words glazed as the glass walls, so shiny we might catch

our true reflections. When He stands to leave
I crest with the wave. Music foams as I flow throng-front,
hope He'll kick-start my crown chakra on His way out.
Sucked into the vortex of bodies in moving meditation,

rhythm whirl-pooling us, sweat and breath, arms hailing
the ceiling—He's torn the portal. Same as any other day
but on Sunday it's Prayer. Afterwards, brothers tithe

trays of shortbread manna, faith-baked cherry pies,
cinnamon roll ambrosia—communion of sugary decadence
(competition for gratitude). Fingers to mouth to belly—
fast gone. *Bhaktis* like me float out,

find trays of crumbs, sent foraging to the kitchen—
crusts and marmalade, butter-glistened knives, hot wire whir
in the gut of the toaster, voltage in my palms.

Back at the ashram, I'm bathroom-girl: sponge porcelain,
slop floors, shine mirrors to shrine-like splendour, shimmy
that smile arranging my lopsided gaze higher.
Don industrial gloves and tackle the handicapped stall
for Gracie, who shits up and down the sides of the bowl.

Line up for Thai tofu stir-fry with eighty other live-ins,
mark a seat for us at the kids' table with my Om scarf
(coyly adjust cleavage). Nate prattles ionized water
or colloidal silver—whatever scheme he's boiling—
he's a salesman on speed, firing faster than we can follow,
while his daughter pees on her seat again.

Outside the rain completes my garden bed. Deer stilt
through aspen, bony shadows guttling
Rupi's snow peas, his yellow beans. We inch toward wary
forest eyes, a field of gentleness. After sunset,

I tuck my girl into her blanket fort, shuffle around
our mess. Try to meditate, pray for more
devotion. Call my mother and get the machine.
Don't tell her I ache

from scrubbing, from shovelling garden dirt,
that rats nest in the walls, grainy urine stench battling
my Nag Champa incense, how someone stole
right into our room, nicked our mini-fridge.

Close Encounters

Three storeys, three long halls—twenty-three doors
on every floor, keys swinging in the locks.

The tub upstairs overflows,
gutters down my bathroom walls.

I wrap the phone cord round my toes, doodle
flowers next to four names on the phone list.

Where have all the virtues gone?
Young girls came, picked every one.

I drag my headboard into the foyer, slap it
against two other abandoned headboards—

noisy things. A door slams and someone screams:
You promised to be celibate with me!

The Master says: anger is a call for love,
jealousy is a call for love, guilt is a call for love.

Skin squeaks on the porcelain tub next door.
Someone sobs down the hall. A kettle boils.

For crying out loud—give it a good squeeze and jiggle it out. It's not a scrotum, it's a *marigold*! We're working to a *schedule*, darling—it must fill and flourish, glorying on The Master's birthday. You've two days, two! Thirteen beds in this ashram so I can't be babying you. This isn't fun and games, sweetheart, this is *service*.

And are we dressed for service? D'you imagine we're off to a *garden party*? You'll be sashaying in the dirt. I say "wear old clothes" and you show up in a *sundress*?

No one here *cares* about your body—and you don't want these neat little granny rows, you're not *crocheting*, you're not knitting *tea cosies*.

This is a catastrophe of boredom—dig it all up and start over, and smoosh them in closer— ignore the how-to tags altogether. I want *abundance*, I want *excess*, think Marie Antoinette. This is an *art form*. The trowel is your paintbrush, so sketch the soil.

No, no, don't scratch like a cat covering its crap—use sweeping strokes, use your whole arm.

Don't do what's *expected*, darling—go *wild*! I want *spirals*, I want *galaxies*, I want Van Gogh. Think colour bridges, think *tiers*. No pansies whimpering in the front row with cosmos tall and whispy in the rear—we don't want your grade school photo.

Wander forget-me-nots like a brook, draw the eye toward my lily pool. People must tumble into the blooms and *disappear* from the world! I'm envisioning watery fairyland mystery, I'm seeing Monet. Come on darling, be daring! Be *outrageous*! Look at me, I mean really—I never do what's *expected*. What d'you guess is under this sarong, Y-fronts? I'm loose and fruity as the spring breeze, darling—it's about letting go of who you *thought* you were. Free yourself from this retro housewife fantasy, strip off your floral and dirty up, darling. Seriously, just take it off and garden in your underwear, garden naked. No one *cares*.

The Master Offers Initiation

God is feminine, plural in the translation—we could say
in the beginning seven sisters created heaven and earth.
It doesn't matter how I teach it—love,

which is God, is the release of perceptual identity,
which is fear. You dream more synapses in your brain
than all the stars in the universe. This is your Big Bang,

the coming together of yin and yang, transfiguration—
would you stop this ecstatic annihilation occurring to your system?
You will become perfect, a new mind. Your ecstasy

is the climax of acceleration—186,000 miles per second
and matter would dissolve. All matter is finally the force of love—
open your heart and part the Red Sea. Teachers of miracles,

it is a new continuum, the awakening from self-identity
to eternity—no definition of yourself can survive
the realization you are whole universal mind. You play

the game of death, but you can't die. You're protecting yourself
from your own illumination—fall apart! The only release
is complete transformation, enlightenment, kundalini

piercing the *ajna*, frenzy of Damascus, the grail...
frigging rising from the tomb! You cross the veil,
you won't be here. And the world will be gone.

Am the good girl

devotee cross-legged at His feet
knees against my back a back against
my knees knees press my thighs
        doped on His drawl
groupie-swooning at His touch
open-throated falling into

His white shirt rising His white shirt
crowd-vanishing
        bust into the eye of the mosh pit
see me see me
        Am a light-junkie
lunatic-high trancing chanting
        ladder to the sky
climb me out

A Devotee's Daily *Seva*

Haggling over hair with my girl—choose Alice band
or barrette, gotta be groomed for townie daycare,
those Salon moms and their diamond nails versus

my thrift shop aura, ashram brand. As usual,
miss car pool, speed like a maniac, highway dematerializing
beneath Rupi's Thunderbird, ploughing past

freshly harvested fields, hay bales like yurts in a commune.
Coffee-jittery and sparrowing every thoughtcrumb,
worrying she'll not be loved well, that they'll toss in

her veggie dog with the worst kind of sausages,
whether her red blanket will be safe from that girl,
if childcare money will appear (or someone will, for me)

miraculously. I'm missing the group reading, not missing
the room's gorgonzola reek, windows moulting plastic
light. He'll be royal on the staircase, ad-libbing

enlightenment, yachting the foyer, patting Gretel's heart chakra.
And I'm flying the back roads, dance version of *Hare Krishna*
praising the cosmos from Rupi's tape deck.

Looping the car park, praying for a spot, wishing brothers
who love it up off-ashram would bloody well carpool.
Skid in through the side door, sway on the mezzanine in meditation,

half-listening to The Master, waiting for the bliss. After Satsang
the music sieves me out the top of my head, separates
the wheat of me from the chaff. But for now I dash

across the street to the Big Cheese Restaurant,
zipping a poodle skirt for noon shift, ready to smile
my heart out at tourists from Chicago. Hoping

Shellie will use her eyes at the waterpark (not stuff
her cheeks with fries, contemplating the slurpy machine,
kids life-jacketless, wailing blue over the rapids).

Saul's baking his cream cheese lasagne. Word's out
and the dinner line's thirty long—he's carnival barking,
sleeves rolled, Christ's biceped face flexing. I fall

into a screaming match mid-dining hall with Krishnan,
captain of the kitchen sparkle roster, rounding up his sailors
with misquotes from The Master. Where's my

"miracle-mindedness"? My "gratitude" (for servitude)?
(Should I sleep in the bloody restaurant too?!)
Later, while my daughter puppy-snores, I flurry off

to the Satsang room, haul out the miracle-minded
vacuum, the hallowed butterfly broom. Toss, stack, line up
three-hundred divinely scattered cushions,

stools, chairs. Gratefully lug bus tubs of consecrated
glasses and mugs, and The Master's cola can (if Jujube hasn't
Holy-Grailed it away, sharing sips of the *Prasad*

with the other high-and-splendids). I sink
into His chair, close my eyes, fill my lungs—
loose the world from all I thought it was. Dump sacred

slipper socks and sweaters in the lost and found.
Maybe sneak upstairs, ask the devi of massage
for a blessed foot rub, fully loosen up.

meditation

outside snow banks
slimed sill height
ice-shod windows sharpen
wall vented air
floorboards hum

under my feet
      in my coccyx
            somewhere
        a scaled sun stirring
someone clicks play
debussy's *clair de lune*
              red tulip unpleating
someone tongues
jyoti jyoti

         fainéant rolling warmth
lushly lidded and rooted
my arms shedding wool
           and branching
their antlered moon

sage smoke quills
a little like the reek of weed
               dirty-sweet
      drifting piano
ascending rachis of prayer

music ripe as the heart
of a peach
to lift us

into the fluted rafters
to lift me
almost
(there is nothing

i want more)
music's voltage
from tailbone to
snap
the window bolt wrenched
a coil of air
goose-pimpling rush

star lid unlatched
a seedpod in time
-lapse and somehow

kneeling
head hinged back
tears pooling
in my ears
the sweetness

oh the sweetness of
sopranoed note
on a glass rim
pinging the rib's bell
that *sound*

  pealing
gulp of air
    face breaching the surface
tension of the room

i don't know how
      to be this
meat cage
    fettered
wedge of grief
after feeling beyond
    the sky's cloth
i sink
face in wet palms

panes frosting
    over
snow melting
into mud

Path to the Inner Sanctum

It's the swoon
    of the hall, lit along the edges
like cinema stairs, my feet glowing

        against oily plush—I give myself
            to this path over and over with an aptitude
for devotion that must be the remnant

                of a past life. But I'm not something
holy, only on my best days
            am I worth saving. Deeper with each footfall,

          boards creaking hollow. What is real
if He says this is a dream? All the sages
              say it too: the veil of Maya—

Sadhus smoking ganja waiting for it to lift,
    dervishes whirling into the center, towards that
pearl of stillness. The floor swings beneath me,

            suspended. Whenever I walk to His room
        there's an unstitching in the chest,
            a loosening in this corset of bones—

    sometimes I wish only a cave,
but who am I fooling, the silence
would eat me whole. The veneer

    walls contract and I'm struck
        with déjà vu. I'm a bell of memory,
            all other visits vibrating against this one.

        A voice fills the shell of my ear, resonant
            and elongated as whale song, He chants
you're looping, looping—let the jar of consciousness

        crack. My body sways, spinal fluid hums—
            perhaps this time
        I'll be remade, undone.

The Foot Massage

Her last lover danced flamenco,
wore voluminous dahlia dresses. Lie back,
she says. I dangle my calves over the edge of her bed—

my daughter's in the dining hall
downstairs with the other kids. Only a thin wall separates
this room and the Guru's visiting room.

She flames a wand of incense, jabs it in a potted palm,
unfolds my cotton flounces. Cross-legged on the rug, she rests
my foot on her thigh. When she parted her lover's thighs

ruffles fanned into flower petals, like the thousand
dala lotus, she says, cunt melting at the center. The muskiness
of sandalwood coils. She oils my foot, twists each toe,

Slicks her thumbs along the arch. Kneads the heel,
spreads oil from ankle to knee, from ankle to—
We're next door to people visiting

The Master. Laughter on the
other side. *Shh*, she says,
and tosses my skirt wide.

Be My Valentine Dear One

Valentine's Day is every day
you allow it to be. Love is a burning fire
within, a singular consciousness—you suffer

from a fatal disease called Limited Perception.
Everyone is terminally ill: I love you
for your ankles, your boobs, for the way

you make me feel. I love you for your new boat,
in defiance of my culture, because you're black
or blue or green. Nobody can give completely

as long as they feel lack. You give to receive, or you give
in sacrifice on the altar of mankind and bathe
the leper's wounds—you don't heal

the incredible sores in your own heart.
When I was a boy we had hate Valentines—
little sheets sent anonymously, saying "I hate you,"

saying awful, awful things. Now we don't bother—
we hate by subtracting from our lives.
How close is love to hate? Right next to it—

*I'm not giving you a Valentine, last year you didn't give back,
and I'll always remember.* You cannot love one thing
and reject something else. Everyone you meet

is a dream of Home. Say *I love you* to somebody
on the street: "What do you mean you love me?
Are you some sort of nut? Here's a dollar, go get a coffee."

Where do you find unity? You've all had beautiful moments:
big swallowtail in the morning grass, pungent mustard
in the meadow, wind rustling the pines, discovering

a tiny wildflower growing out of a crevice in a rock.
What else would you finally be but Divine?
There is nothing outside of you—you are the rock,

the plant, the rich brown earth we will harvest from.
Are you afraid to go to the altar and reveal
what you really think about yourself?

Of course you're afraid. That's why you're
here. Take my hand, we'll go together.
Let me love you tonight.

Am the new shiny handbag

plume in the fedora
two-door with a high-gloss finish
chauffeur me round
            by the elbow
watch my hips swing
               get sprung
Am your spaniel
watch me come
           by myself
watch me lie
       the length of your tub
watch me stir your Dutch coffee
lekker
      watch me slurp

Dorm Room 214

Under the blown glass angels with gold-dipped heads strung up by
their haloes, a poster of Rossetti's *Lilith*, Klimt's *Kiss*, all magpied
from The Barn—our swap shop, where almost anything you
imagine miraculously appears soon after you think of it. Like the
soda shoppe chair in front of the window where the Pole likes to
fuck me, at night, with the lights on. And the sprawling threadbare
chaise behind the gauzy sarong wall, where one night, three of
us completely ignored Kubrick's *Eyes Wide Shut*, discovered what
yoga was really for—two Aussie girls and that French cyclist with
River Phoenix hair. This Dutch guy says my place reminds him
of a Turkish bazaar, a harem, a Babylonian shrine. He likes to
play harmonica in the shower, admire his chest in that mosaiced
mirror above the sink, where the German wrote *ich liebe dich* with
my daughter's alphabet stickers, and I thought German had a dirty
ring. Half the place bed-hops. So hard to say no. To say no seems...
ungrateful. Like refusing Godiva's chocolates, silk wedding saris,
a foot massage. The ashram in-words: *merci* and *oui, tak, ja, sí, surebaby.*

A Devotee's Daily Salvation

On Tuesdays the whole ashram lets go
of its slingshot aimed at heaven.
                    Me and my girl
sleep late, wash our hair in the tub, flip pancakes
in the kitchen, sloth through service. I pray

we don't score that front-desk call (jubilant,
expectant):
                "Dear One's here!"
Ride the personal guilt bus to the foyer—
seven days blessed should feel like bliss, yes?

The Master stops, rests His elbow on my shoulder,
His idioms graze my collar bones, words flung like a net—
shampoo, something fruity. I trail him to Satsang,

cat in at His feet, spine warming. His mind speed-fires,
shakti-electric, and soon I'm overcharged, leaking lithium.
Jess shoulder-taps me, smiles—
                            my romp with the kids.
Skip to the horsie swings suped up

on chi, chase four soft kitten heads squealing snowlight,
parka hoods bobbing at their necks. Kick with them
into the welkin,
                over and over into cowlicks of cloud.

*

Wrangle your own lunch day, elbow to elbow
in the kitchen for the post-meditation ravening,
too many brothers and no rostered cooks.

I slice cucumber onto end crusts, child hip-slouched.
Someone's scoffed our tofu slices, our soy cheese,
Sharpied and stashed in back of the walk-in,

everyone's eaten the communal loaves
and no one's washing anything. I'm on kitchen clean up,
ingratitude hanging
                    like a bat.

I tack a note on the Brotherhood Board,
tracking our pilfered fridge.
                              Hog three laundry machines—
lights and darks and sheets all spinning

time into a longer cloth. Little one dragging
her xylophone-on-wheels, meandering
Twinkle Twinkle by ear.

*

Pasta surprise whipped up by Priya,
fairy of thrift—frigid and gummy leftover
creamed corn, overripe tomatoes. I butter toast,

ask Wiktor to crack open a jar of Smucker's—
he's wolfing pasta—Priya flutters around him, says
it's a miracle what we can do

from our place of peace.
                               My child curls in my lap.
I inhale the grunginess of her hair.
Unwashed for a week, it smells like home.

Nate

That tap water you're giving your kid? Acidic, you know. Dicey stuff. You think it's hydrating but it's boosting cancer growth, it's razing DNA. We don't want *these* kids downing crap. Check 'em out—Holy untainted angel pure! Hailey—

yolk in your belly, baby. Filtered water's okay, but the body hankers for alkaline. Slide me the ketchup, will you? The Ionizer doesn't just alkalize—it infuses silver particles. D'you know colloidal silver? That's what we want inside our kiddies. Not just immune support, I'm talking molecular change, total transformation. But colloidal gold— that's the kundalini ticket, shells your crown like a peanut. Has other *stimulating* benefits too, not that you'd need that. Hailey, carrots—dunk 'em in the sauce,

good girl. You'll see it in your face. It's rebuilding cells, it's reversing aging—basically collapsing time. We're using it on Hailey—that gum thing? Money hasn't manifested yet, but it will, it will for sure, and it's looking pretty healed now anyway. So it's also anti-parasitical, scouring your insides. But if we wanna talk parasites, colloidal copper's the weapon, like drinking pennies. I've got to tell you...

no, I can't tell you what came out of this body. Frightening what's riding our intestines. Average North American's got four pounds of undigested meat caking his bowels and you know what that breeds—sci-fi micro-horror. Way we treat our bodies is a metaphor for how we treat each other—greedy or withholding, fulfilling cravings rather than needs. But flesh heals fast when we supply this liquid aid. Hey, pudding's out.

Come on, Hailey—green one's your dish. I'll deliver some water to your room tonight, okay? After her bedtime stories and snuggles. Twelve bucks a pop, but I'll spring *you* a sweet deal.

Am the villain the scourge

of my womb
crossing my line of faith crossing
the zealot's picket line
carnival signs freak-show grotesque

forced contractions like a pumping fist
just a little puff of air he says
spotlessly white-coated (knife in the pocket)

Am living with the cryptic
                    itch of dismemberment
won't remember that plump leg
won't hold
            the eyes
won't ever

What we Learn in Childhood

I wake from a howling
darkness, dream-claws raking floor—
I'm four years old. Storm quakes
the bottle-glass panes; a drainpipe empties wildly.
She appears by my bed, my grandmother. A vision
outlined in window flash, brushes damp fringe from my face.
Her dry hands spark with static and the sky lamps again.
She rocks me through the hall's shifting ghosts,
blowing them back into those cobwebbed and wiry spaces
between the walls, empties me
from her arms into the mothy bed of familiar smells—mulled
pouch tobacco, sharp mints, grimy tang of coal.
The clock ticks on the mantle, my granddad snores,
ceiling chain-pull magically clicks the room grey.

And I wake choking a scream, hinge upright on my futon,
lungs sucking air, basement ghost salamandering away—
it envelopes under the door and the keys in my lock jangle.
Rain rages staccato against our palisade of windows,
pine arms in belled cuffs shadow-puppet the screens.
I stumble into her alcove, cluttered behind a curtain,
all the stuffed creatures lightening-eyed, then dark again.
She's sprawled under her blankets, furred
in the animal sleep of a four-year-old,
one arm and leg noodling the floor.
I tuck the wayward limbs and umpteenth-guess

my choice to cross the Pacific. Will she ever feel
how I felt in my grandparent's bed—
those spells of sound safety?

Harry

He's got my grandfather's lilt to the left, tool belt
slumped to one side, yesteryear shadows strung
like helium balloons from his torso, swaying, cawing.
His forearm on the doorframe, scoping my room
over my head, faint grit of solder fluxing
from his denim. Mortar and pestle knuckles,
smile like a cracked geode, cave of agate
darkly glassing.
            Throat nicked, oxidised,
telling me each galloping footfall, every song
and howl from my child agitates below, nettles
the walls. At first they dug into his skull,
those wallops and bellows, tracked through
dreams—kids swinging truck tires, rutting his ceiling
with dress-up heels.
            Didn't like to complain
so each day he knelt, prayed. And then a revelation—
all that squalling, every rollick and wail
was joy. Joy! Now he basks in the felicity of sound,
her squeals are his music, his elysian booze.
He's been wondering why I don't play
tunes, lifts a nineties boom box from the hall—
mined from the dumpster, wires tweaked
and fused now, double cassette, CD and radio,
speakers scotch-smooth. Says my joy is his joy.

The Guru's Feet

Today The Master's socks don't match. Same shade of washed-out denim, but one sock's thinly ribbed and the other's a pearl weave. I'm on my knees in the main foyer, and His toes almost touch my jeans. He's laughing with Cliff—my shoulder blade rests against Cliff's shin. Cliff's a psychiatrist, but everyone calls for prescriptions like he's a GP. He wrote up antibiotics for my abscessed tooth, birth control for Lorelei. Everyone crowds in until I'm twelve o'clock in a circle around The Master. He tickles the top of my head, lazily, almost sensually, so I have no idea what He's saying. My head's sparking and His flat Chicago accent umbrellas me.

Then He springs back and the circle widens. He pinches the fabric of His jeans at the thighs and hikes them mid-calf, skips toodle-oo backwards down the hall, blue peepers and baldy head shining. The crowd peels, bodies press against walls to make room, everyone whooping with glee, cheering His veiny-legged jig as if He's Lord of the Dance. He casually whacks Yasmyn on the crown as he passes; Yasmyn, with wild hair extensions and her one-note Billie Holiday scream. Her irises slot-machine and she sinks to her knees, braids in a Medusa-gyre. Those either side get off on her light-climax, one eye on Him, hoping He'll spot how worthy they are, burn them with *shaktipat* too. But now He's playing silly faces with Athena. They were supposedly screwing in the early days, but I've barely been here a year so I don't know much about anything.

Except that Athena shook me by the shoulders in the laundry room, accused me of too many lovers in a row. Had me confess a few, crowned me slutty. The Master fashioned her after the Greek goddess, but her real name's something like Vicky. Used to blow dope smoke out her living room window so her toddler wouldn't choke it in. Had a cartload of beaus too, says her daughter, eighteen now and part of the mob. The eye-gazing between The Master and Athena drags out—a meeting of almost-equals. Finally her chin sips skywards and her lids hummingbird-blur.

He giddy-ups, His mis-matched feet hitch-stepping towards the Satsang room where He'll recline in His La-Z-Boy, perform for the sheeping crowd. He's mumbling something about string theory, and I've no idea what, because I'm stretched onto my toes, noodle-thin, mind emptying, arms lifting. I trip forward, wayward as a wind-born chip packet, my toes catching each kink in the carpet, on course to His feet.

II

Don't go unveiled into that valley of Manyoon:
every grain of sand there is an atom of desire.

—Ghalib, translated by Adrienne Rich

Am the nymph of the breast

spindling wishes at the wheel
of her watery opal nipple
am lost in my own mouth
swanning the polished brook
pilgrim of the holy doorway

Am the curve the crook
the splendid bow the glistening
rose the mirror of my own
amrita
      am plunging into
brambled darkness
ruined and grateful

Chronicles of Seeds and Dust

I'm driving into snow's white noise, away from her cabin, the sky's still half-lit—I used to stay until dawn. Quarter-sized flakes splat the windshield, the wipers quarrel furiously—pelage of snow so densely furred I can't tell where the sun is setting. A pair of speckled pippi shells dangles on a string from my rear view, pecan-stained as an Aussie tan, spooning each other.

*

I walk naked into Mirror Lake, every pore pimpling against the descent. Translucent sheets of red pine pollen marble the surface. The wind takes form as it whisks through the trees unspooling pollen midair (long hair out a car window flying against the blurring sky). Laughter breaks loose from a houseboat on the far side of the lake, a straggle of voices begins *Happy Birthday*, most of them find the same key. When I lift my arms a fine yolky powder coats my skin. I kick onto my back, scull my hands to stay afloat, wait for the current to carry me.

*

Up this high it's not so hot, but my tears feel mysterious as the urge to eat cotton candy and ride the Ferris wheel. It stops for people below and the chair rocks like a tin dinghy on a wave. The lake tucks neatly into the nape of the land, small town suburbs scatter to trailer parks and farms. Ferris wheels in Australia overlook the beach: highways of yellow sand, surfers straddling their boards beyond the breakline, oiled bikini bodies, kids, collies, ice cream van. The wheel drops past the chrome gate, past the queue of tourists. A rush of warm air dries my cheeks. I stuff my mouth with aerated sugar. Where I come from we call it fairy floss.

*

Only seven bucks at Wally's Fall Sale, this palm-sized porcelain replica of Canova's *Cupid and Psyche*, white beneath the dust. Wally lifts his jelly-roll paunch, shuffles sideways between shelves of retro flatware and Depression glass to ask me if I've found what I'm looking for. I tell him I don't know what I'm looking for. He nods at the statue in my hand, says, *We're all lookin' fer love, honey.* The wind swings the door wide, tinkling the bell. A tail of rusty leaves whips in.

Marjeta

So I tell Ava I am liking Gavain, and asking for her to keep my secrets, you understand? Then she is planning motorbike with him. With Gavain! To picnic Mirror Lake! And I am the smashing egg in pantry, yolk all over floor—why does she telling me at waitress shift when it is expecting of me to be so happy? She is pulling me into pantry,

whispering like smoking girl in church asking to meet for some drags. Then saying probably she is kissing the man of my love today, one man in whole of ashram. So my secret to her she is just forgetting—poof! And I am trying with my hard work to be not crying, but Ava sees my tears and makes ugly smelling bad milk face, and just then leaves. Like that—gone!

Not "gone" like flash out of physical world into white of the heaven, just "gone" like leaving so quickly with her feet. There can be no heart in her chest, I am telling you what is certain empty. And I am here in quiet pantry like the little kitten, not good for speaking, just waah-waah, and Captain Kelly comes talking like the actor reading from paper: "you are telling yourself the story, blah-blah, the story it is who you are not, blah-blah"

—forget this blah-blah! I feel true to be crying if inside is the stone of pain and then the story washing away. But that Ava, oh biggest story of my life—all the butter hair swish-swish, and always she is eating huge dish of food like the fat man, and staying long stick bug.

But this is important story, because The Master saying so clearly we go to the *mukti* in pairs, like old ark story, but boy-girl, not giraffe-giraffe. Don't worry, I'm sure girl-girl and boy-boy okay too. And I am certain these weeks ago I am finding my pair. And what a stupid mouth to be secreting my love, making her eyes looking at him in freshness.

Now on motorbike seat she is pressing this private of her body against his bottom, the Gavain of my love, and her Ava hands tight on his ah so sexy stomach. And now I am angry villain of my mind because Captain Kelly stops my wash-away crying. Sometimes we must be forgetting awakening and having the biggest river of cry. But for awakening we must first have the pair. This is clearly told by The Master and my huge worry.

A Devotee's Daily Chastity

Deliver my girl in pre-stained clothes—
rostered childcare with Nate and Jay.
Full-body painting, full-body craft,

kids flour-gluing tissue paper to arms—voila! Fairy wings!
But instead of child-free Satsang bliss, I'm giggling

through a double shift with Chris.
Someone asks why all the tofu on the menu?
Chris says, "It's in season." I'm snort-laughing,

over-relaxing, taking liberties (I'm coveting)—
might be a past life thing, a given if it wasn't for his

spouse. People ask if I'm a Brit, South African,
Kiwi, Canadian—*Yes!* I say. *Have you been there?*
I get flirty/silly, spill a bowl of beer cheese soup
in a Dad's plaid lap. I'm off-kilter,

serve cream sodas instead of shakes, stick my thumb
in someone's flan, pour dressings
in the wrong containers, forfeit my break.

*

Mock tuna dinner with my small mud-creature—
gardening today. She's got a shrivelled worm
in her pocket and a sword-shaped stick.

Kids hate the fake fish salad, play elves and orcs
up and down the main hall, sticks thwacking,
feet muddying until Priya loses her place of peace,

rounds them up with a broom. I scuttle to and from
the men's loos with toilet paper towers, urinal cakes,
leave Priya to mediate kids plus the desire for peace;

smile demurely/timidly at the devi of massage
as she passes—she misses me posing
behind my wedding cake of bathroom supplies.

*

After my little one drifts off,
I slink into my halter-top, meet Wiktor
in the Satsang room. Cringe/glow each time

he calls me Chicky-Babe in his wolfish accent, laugh
as he vacuums with his butt stuck out,
laugh when he asks "Whaat? Whaat?"

We stack cushions and chairs, Cranberries blaring,
dancing into a sweaty hypno-trance. I let him

spin me dizzy, my teensy skirt flaring
horizontal, let him hoist my hips,
slide me down his chest, over his

abs, over and over his hard abs. Let my skirt flooze
past my bum each time I slide, my fingers

skulking his loose curls. Let him lift me
out of my head, fly me with the music—wonder

why he never asks me to a movie,
wonder if he's still celibate,
if this is sex for him.

Am the pedal and the seat

a sweaty bare-skinned ride
hintern? arsch? what did he say?
        shhh don't speak
that guttural language of desire
lungs humph and mouth smacks
hefted like a sack of wheat
kneaded salted flayed
one stubble-burned moment of release
and the whoa of time

lips hunting my lobe
smoky lamp-lit sky
          fading
      strange tongue
     distract me
this is not it never it

Self Portrait

The child hides in her mother's tulle-
whipped row of thrift-shop ball gowns.

Three gold rings on the bathroom vanity—
none with diamonds.

Guru's photo in a key-chain frame,
his come-hither smile on the child's nightstand.

Fact (found in a locked diary): *men's feet, not their noses,*
are comparable to the size of their fruit.

The child trails her mother from keyhole to
keyhole, rat-a-tat-tatting for sitters.

Two carefully lost items: a kazoo
at a playground, lacy knickers on a lover's bed.

Polaroid of the Guru's feet on the bedroom wall.
The diamond is in the heart, He says.

The mother applies mascara in the hall mirror.
The child strokes the prickles on her mother's legs.

What's the point of a big dick

if you don't know how to use it?
His ex blurts this at dinner,
mid-dining hall, then half-laughs
while those nearby fidget dishes,
wind pasta round their forks.
He swigs soda, thigh-nudges me
under the table. Serves him right
for bragging—always Michael Jacksoning
his crotch, going on about
the black gene in the Dutch, anosmic
to the racist whiff of his words.
Now she's fleeing for the washrooms,
napkin-dabbing her sweater. I follow
and he grins, thinking she's gonna get it—
            but I want to ask her
if he used meditation to avoid
talking, if he went AWOL for weeks,
if they made love only after showering,
if it drained him to come—sluggish at gigs,
blaming sex, blaming her. If he ever
went down on her. I want to know
if he ever bought her dinner, gave her gifts
he wanted for himself. If it was the
Al Green covers, his blues
harmonica, dark eyes liquid
under the stage lights, huge
hands gripping the mic.

A Devotee's Daily Penance

Me and Sebastian (my periodic butterfly),
pinned to the childcare roster, so itchy
for a Satsang hit we usher the girls across the hall
to the whoops following The Master.

He's ten feet away, sermoning over one shoulder,
crowd turkey-tailing behind. The girls squeal
and He turns, hunches His body, smiles like a realtor.
His granddaughter waddles up, offers a cheek.

My child freezes. He points
Look at the light in this one! Look how bright!
Everyone *ooo's* and *ahh's* and He nods our way,

makes a quip about the height of Dutch men.
We're both so elated to be seen we say *gezellig*
to feeding ducks at the lake. Four-year-old

footprints disappearing into the clay, glossy
surface sucking itself smooth. Until the magic
fades and we're dragging hungry mud-splattered
babes. Up the back stairs to the washrooms,

satsang over, other brothers still humming
on His wattage, music and bodies roiling—
my shade detaches from heel tips, drifts
towards that nucleus of *bhava* ecstasy.

*

When I drop off my girl, Chris's wife emerges
from her cyber-world to quiz me
on my love life. I glance at her husband's gold band, say,

all the good ones are taken.
Six months into their marriage she wooed
spiritual celibacy. He's Canadian, she's Kiwi,
so ixnay on the green cards.

Chris'll feed my child protein shakes,
surf cable cartoons, play hide and seek.
And I'll scoop ice cream for other folks' kids,

squeeze mustard into hexagonal jars,
stack plates on my arms with the finesse
of a circus juggler, smile, smile, smile. Rush

home to serve restaurant veggie burgers
to my child plus one—babysitting trade-off.
Play *Candyland* and let them cheat
their skillfully crinkled cards.

*

Before bed, I mop the main foyer,
swivel my hips in time with the flow,
get a mambo rhythm going—my feet glide,
the mop slides. I'm the salsa mopping mamma.

I daydream about teaching again in the fall,
practice barres and a sprung floor, mirrors
trebling rows of ribboned slippers in tendu,
piano tinkling a simpler world. A night breeze

salts my sweat, the front door swings.
Wiktor and Ivy stroll to a film,
fingers knotted. She's American, he needs

a green card, it's fated. He'll be dancing with me
next week, for sure. I slop the polished cement,
smear it grey to black.

Am an outline of a woman

aura around a shadow
constellation punched and hung high
divination in the night sky
wyrd

Am wanting
          not to want
to be hollowed out
              hallowed
looted scooped and carved
lit like a jack-o-lantern
soothsaying
luminous

Dottie-Anne

Come sit while you wait your turn, good girl, good. You could be
my daughter, don't you think? Look at our locks—probably buy
the same hair-dye, wink-wink. Same heavy lids too. Bit shadowed
and baggy under the eyeballs—Nate says parasites, but don't you
believe his filthy mouth.

Guess what's hiding in these boxes,
honey? Day-olds from the German Bakery! Iced and jellies, but
it's off to Vespers for this batch—grab a few for your pretty
li'l precious. Shh, and we'll both scoff an itsy-bitsy right now.
You're with me, no one'll say peep. Who doesn't love fried
cakes, please tell me! Take a powdered too, tuck 'em in this *TV
Week,* I'm done. Couldn't we eat a whole box of these tempters!
You know, I could adopt you honey—

fix all your troubles.
I'm one-hundred percent for real! Then you'd be a genuine
U.S. citizen, and li'l precious would be my grandkiddy, should
have a nearby granny—tragical. Gotta scrap this green card
lottery scam, don't you think? Never a winner! Look at that
dog's line of illegals,

all losers! Immigration nabs aliens this way—
more entries from us, the more suspicious. Best to be hush-hush
or it comes down on the ashram. Can't have them fine-tooth-
combing our student paperwork. You wanna bring it down

on Dear One's back? You folks can't be stacking more on his shoulders. He's got to flood the Teaching into the whole damn world! Who else'll be the goddamned saviour, please tell me! You don't see it,

all you frilly twenties gals from hot places hitching up your hooker tops in the middle of Satsang. You all brassy show-offs, *me-me-me*, ungrateful. And greedy. All like *teenagers*. Cartload of divas with your hands out and legs open. Didn't even thank me for the doughnuts, did you? Got nothing to say with a mouth full of cake, have you honey? Nuts if you think I'd adopt one of you. Nuts! Take them treats and off you go, greedy tart.

A Devotee's Daily Transformation

Wiktor and Ivy, shoulder to shoulder
in the Reading Room, Connie reads: "...peace
peace, bosh-bosh-bosh." Ivy—who sleeps

same floor as The Master's visiting room, who never
lifts a broom, transcribes His videos as service,
gunslinging the teachings, bloodlust

curling her lip—now threading Wiktor's fingers,
lids lowered like she's soaking rays from the overheads.
We funnel into Satsang after The Master. I choose

the raised dais behind His chair for the finest view—
are their fingers super-glued?
Shellie arrives, notices me noticing.

I close my eyes, suck air through one nostril—
my head's concrete. Meditation music cranks,
Shellie drags me center, rubs my temples,

tugs the hair at my crown until I blow
apart like a seed puff, cry it out.
And they all bundle in, all the light freaks:

Gloee and Ana, Lorelei and Sebastian, Blair scooting in,
headphones necklaced, cord trailing. Blair's boy, Jan
and his Austrian girl on the side, both breathy-slender,

Rupi, saronged and serene. And Wiktor,
always circle's core, arms rocketing. I'm pressed
against his back, and I know he knows it's me.

He inhales my mind and lifts me with him
—a pituitary trick we've practiced dancing,
like flexing the muscles that move the ears;

the warm bud of awareness halfway
to ecstasy, the small explosion that follows.
Someone parts the curtains,

sunlight swells so godly
I lose track of why I'm crying,
of how I'm here.

*

Over at the restaurant Ana zips me
into a 40's low-back dress, her wrist on my neck,
tucking my bra straps, shirt buttons straining

against her breasts—sensory world slamming
into me, always. Ana knots my apron, tucks a ticket book.
I cloud through the restaurant's sky and she shadows me,

bussing tables I don't recall waiting on.
The whole place seems empty, soundless,
but as the afternoon lands, chatter begins to hiss

like espresso steam, and my heels ache.
Ivy leads Wiktor in for an Italian soda, they pose
at the coffee bar, Ivy cracking her invisible whip,

nixing *Chicky-Babe*, Wiktor's Colgate smile
cockeyed, his horsey laugh. Some things
less dazzling in daylight.

The Guru's Granddaughter

Who can fault her after five years as gossamer
fairy of the ashram, as indigo star-child,
wee pussy willow, saffron Sadie,
everybody's Kewpie doll baby—
you'd think there weren't thirty-six other kids
dogging the halls
                        in their swap-shop hand-me-downs.
Her anointed parents meander about hands-free—
Daddy with Fender slung across his chest,
Mommy with her buttercup cheeks
and a doughnut in her pocket, whacked out
on that glossy lolly-high of celebrity.
Devotee babysitters vulturing, vying
for the honour. While other parents
scrape out the deep fryer, crank
the industrial dishwasher, haggle childcare,
trade off to meditate, to sit with Him.
                        She swings between
two sitters, playing *one-two-three-jump,*
frilled up in gingham and bows,
telling the others, telling everyone, *My Grandpa*
is the light of the world!

Saul

Yeah yeah, I know it, they all of 'em adore me,
'specially them small ones, they always running up screaming, *Sauly!*
Sauly! Play with us Sauly. C'mon, c'mon, take us for a ride
on your motorcycle, Sauly. They get attracted to my light, you know—
same squall every place I go, I'm like flypaper.
    Skipping down the hall bawling after me,
        Sauly, we love you Sauly! Li'l munchkins.

You got a sweet one, for sure. Looks like that baldy kid
    off *The Matrix* which can bend spoons, you know?
Sure got a cutesy drawl, that kid o'yours. Here's a hoot—they was all
        streaking round the Satsang room the other afternoon, crawling
        behind the stage, up the walls, yours and the rest, dragging blanket-capes
like pint-size super heroes. And Priya's doing the blonde doll,
        losing her shit, yelling for 'em all to get back
    in what they was wearing. And yours pipes up, *I'm allowed to be nudey*

in Australia, heh-heh-heh. They all drop their capes, bolt off squealing, falling over their pinkies—them pip-squeak tooshies, heh-heh-heh.

Got gall, your one...yeah-yeah, sure, I'll keep an eye— but just 'til four. When's your shift done? 'Cause I'm manning the AA meeting up at the Healing Center, then a *ren-dez-vous* at the pool hall. Wish I could help more—got alota balls in the air. Busy guy! Hey, I'll haul her by for a soda so she don't miss you so bad, my treat.

I'm a big softy for them li'l mischief-makers. I'm all heart when it comes to them butterballs, they get me right *here*.

Grandmother Dream

She waits in the subconscious blur of my room,
my granddad at her shoulder like a familiar,
his hands blackened with engine grease,

fingerprinting the sleeve of her floral dress.
She wards my meditation cushion, waits for dawn to crack
my mind like a bird shell. In her palms

a wheel of greased memory; weathered book
from the shelf of my childhood—tale about a garden,
about youth blithely gobbling all it fancies.

She wears one scuffed brown slipper, one fur-trimmed green,
wears her apron like the uniform of a wife,
her auburn hair like a hedge witch. She unfolds

the linen depths of her apron to reveal
a mound of herb scones, knob of melting butter,
says: *Careful what you eat in a dream.*

She sets a table in the dining cart of a train,
heading for the Blue Mountains out of Sydney—
I'm on the wrong train, heading to Chicago,

watching her through two windows, her train
shrinking into the distance. I'm heading from Regina
across the Rockies, pine needles scratching the glass—

the glass of my bedroom window. She sits in the frame,
one leg crossed, fur slipper dangling. The sun
rising behind her. She holds dawn

on her spine in a blaze of wings. Offers a wheel of water,
a bowl deep enough to wash memory.
She waits for me to remember

why she's not gone, waits for me to wake
and wash my face. My hands shake, black with grease,
fingerprinting my cheeks, eyelids, my long Buddha lobes.

This bowl of holy water for me to bless
my child, my precious breath, my pulse,
my holy neglect, wholly forgotten

with a sitter, in daycare, running wild in the garden,
clad in the garments of an inborn story. A book opens
from the shelf of my childhood,

a tale about matches and a girl tiptoed in snow,
peering through windows at what she cannot have.
My grandmother kneels on the quilt

she stitched into my story. She warms my feet
with a handful of matches. She's waiting for the thawing,
waiting for me to crack open like the dawn.

Dragon Woman

Her ears curve lobeless and pointy, seriously elfish,
    like *Lord of the Rings* prosthetics,
and when she teaches I resist
    a reach-out-and-flick itch. Everyone's rapt—
        she's been on retreat so long her words flow

ferocious and juicy. When I first saw her, yesterday,
        those lizard orbs strobed me—
a fibre-optic gaze so penetrating
    my balloon popped. Wasn't near tears
    the moment before—candled in concentration,

    widening to the room, pranayam circling smooth,
then an odd impulse to slip out of practice, glance
    at the stools by the window. And she's honing
        into me. Wings unfold
    behind her, scaled and greased, scalloped

crest of radiance where a halo might be.
And I'm heaving out the top of my head, legs buckling
as I lift. She palms my jeans and tugs
my mind back into this world, hauls a Niagara Falls
lode down my spine, so full I gag—

like in the moment of birth when the head maws you wide.
Fuel bursts the marma points, veins fleshy
and blood-drunk, and I'm throned
in the centre of my skull, straining
towards a pinprick of light, uncoupling...

She releases me, and like a scene-change on a fly bar
I drop from the rigging, canvas bolting to the stage,
still flapping at the tower. She's gone,
the room's mostly empty,
and I'm no longer His.

Am the house of neglect

haunting my room
                       the almost-
jewel of nacre dust
she plays dollies she draws she hums
she watches TV watches me
watching myself

am a dress-up mirror
                    she plays
in my chemise and panties sets
loose silky skins
the bagginess of silence
              my devotee
my copycat

The Master Attempts to Christen Me

Morning slices me through vertical blinds—
one eye dark. He tenders liquorice allsorts,
five of us kneel in His room, sugared on the *prasad*
of His proximity. He measures me,
there's a tone he gets:

> *Looks to me like a Dolores, doesn't she*
> *carry herself like a Dolores? Used to be*
> *a dancer—suits her, don't you think?*

They bob their heads yes-yes-yes,
a line of jack-in-the-boxes.
He eyes me sideways and winks, it seems
at my breasts. Could be worse:

> *Krispy, Tutti, Sprinkles, Stretch,*
> *JackPot, Poppins, Gloee, Great Ray,*
> *Lambie, Lillums, Doubtless, Dude,*
> *Funny Boy...*

Supposed to wash away the precious
identity, Solomon's seal
of His approval (or a way for Him
to remember all our names).

I once ran a healing centre
and people tried calling me Amethyst—

some Aussie medium channelling
an archangel declared it my star-name,
a kind of spiritual glamour, like forking out
for a tattoo of a Sanskrit mantra.

All through the ashram, later,
brothers call me
Dolores—I walk on, make a face,
with my fingers make a cross.

III

to be possessed or
abandoned by a god
is not in the language

—John Thompson

Who is The Master?

I am the Good Shepherd. I am a catalyst of light. I am at the Alpha and the Omega point in time. I am the music of the spheres. I am part of a species that's evolving to galactic identity. I am offering you a flow of reality. I am offering you total release. I am converting form. I am transforming your individual thoughts. I am a continual intrusion. I know how your minds work. I've broken you out of the pattern of your own sequential thinking. Because I can sow everything, I can reap everything. I am resolving the problem. This is the lifting of the veil. You need a saviour. No one could love you more than I do. I am the Universe. And I'm looking right at you.

Scopaesthesia

Stepping over the frozen tombs of dead
insects, ring pulls, lost hairclips—her morning
walk ices with the weather. Legs dragging

yesterday's corridors, conversation's
quicksand floors. She watches her mind
but there's no reigning it in.

Water an oiled palette of sky
and willow, each green-draped arm, weep
of cloud held torpid within the rimed shore.

A shadow skirts the fringe
then veers; something crunches behind
crimping her nerves. She scans the bushes,

treetops, watches herself watching
nothing. Boots guzzled in mud,
she angles her chin over the mirror—

shock swallows a reflexive cry—
her grandmother's eyes, fiery
locks cockled and floating, her face

spooking from beneath
the lake's glass, spectres stirring
around her, milky and familiar.

A gust ravels life, branches skim
the air like wings, something snaps.
She's not dreaming. She's stumbling

up the trail, shedding weight—
vein of disbelief, blade of cynicism—
spectres breaching the water's skin,

wildly shapeshifting—
mother-child-sister-self—
swooping after her.

A Devotee's Daily Gratitude

Athena's balling out a newbie for sitting arms crossed,
he's not open, he's defensive and shut down, he's never
gonna get this, may as well fly back home to Florida—
sure rosy not to be a newbie anymore. I can peel

my own portal, just need to shut my eyes, exhale
through the top. Exhale, exhale,
just keep my damn eyes shut, arms up and
she'll think I'm with her, might not even see me.

Waitressing in thirty, gratitude
often opens my head—what am I grateful for?
Come on, what? What? I'm waiting

for my childcare, waiting for Cliff to hang up
the emergency phone, he's chuckling away.
Childcare's clearly bailed and forgiveness isn't

on the restaurant menu. I race the dorm halls,
daughter at my heels, rapping on the regular doors. Chris
lugs a busted box, acoustic guitar case, piggybacks
a beat up electric, his greasy bed-hair screaming

womanless. Soon-to-be-ex-wife crated her cyberland,
relocated to post-terrorist New York, planning
to open a sister-ashram and deliver the city.
He's moving in two rooms down, sorry he can't sit.

My child's hand nudges into mine—I think of
Ana and Marjeta, heels clicking into the kitchen,
aproning their midriffs—

                    she tugs me towards the playground,
and I mentally ditch my shift. She makes me skip
the whole way, makes me swoop with the swallows.

We snake-tunnel the sand, her fluffy hair
nets sunlight, her fingers so busy and sandy.
She smiles, looks up into my eyes.

Inside the Peel

People snap open bananas and the fruit
spills in pre-cut portions
onto tabletops, into palms, bowls of bananas
sliced inside their skins. Uncanny

after finding myself prone on the rug,
no memory of lilting over
during meditation, my mind a summer sky—

endless and bright. And the usual thought train,
that line of rusty boxcars,
has stopped. All my worries, my stories,

my foibles, hover like a puff of cloud
in the unbound mind,
and it's not a decision, there's no

attachment, so it lifts off—gone.
A magnificent emptiness envelops me,
or maybe I am the emptiness, and the body
appears to be crying—watery eyes open

and the world's a thin rind of matter
shaped around that same vast emptiness;
later I'll call it Peace. I rise and enter

the dining hall, stepping softly
upon the shell of the world, all the other bodies
lustrous, glowing like silk lampshades.
High above the fluorescents flicker

and the room echoes dusk by the river, air
lit with firefly lanterns, fiery bodies
nibbling small circles of food, fingers red-edged
like a hand held to the sun—

and then the jolt. I question
the pre-cut fruit. No one else seems to realize—
they eat and peel and eat as if bananas always

fall out in pieces, but I remember
sticking the needle in each yellow spine,
sweeping that thin foil of metal,

slicing the day's dessert
at one-inch intervals, transforming them inside
their own skins, a faint line of holes

the only evidence. Me and Chris in the kitchen
crafting the mystery, laughing,
imagining their faces when they open
the bananas, but no one's surprised—

all lost in their own prayerful highs.
Someone asks, *Are these plantains?*
No, we used a needle. And slowly
the light blithers out of everything.

Midnight in the Dining Hall

Chris invites me to share leftovers:
an oyster mushroom from his fork to my lips,

that tinny half-smell of stale smoke
wafting off his waiter's shirt, it's wine-splashed cuff.

I'm still in ballet-ma'am tights, sweater flirting
up my thighs. I don't need to worry

if he minds me nibbling off his plate, if I'm eating
too much—it's as if we've always dined this way.

We lose ourselves in the pleasure
noises, the delectable silences.

We've been friends three years, but tonight
we're feeding each other marinated tofu,

dripping lemongrass coulis, my fork in his mouth.
His gaze rolling over my leotard cleavage

on its way to the plate. We discard our utensils,
mop up sauce with our fingertips.

Am the scarlet A

stitched to his chest
my hand in his hand
and his hand in my hand
        our public confession

(they mumble in corners
say she's fickle she's fey
pathological she'll leave you heartsick
and hammered in the crotch)

Am the scuttlebutt mongrel
        dish in the dirt
shot in the breeze

You totally fall in love with their light, I mean take Mike, he's what, *fifty*? And Luca, with the metal bitsies and fat hole-thingys, and through the *nipple*? Must have been the light. But you use it up too quickly, then, news-flash— a new one! Are you working through the phone list? I mean,

leave some for the rest of us! Problem is you've no stick-to-it-*intuitiveness*. I'm your *friend*, so I should tell you everyone's talking. (I'm talking.) Kinda been building. Like, you were dancing with Wiktor and Józef upstairs at The Cheese, and they're twirling you silly, passing you to and fro in a very *handsy* way like they're, god, *sharing* you? I don't wanna know, but why not sit a few out? Other gals got dance cards to fill!

And now Chris...he's not *divorced* yet. It's a bit murky, and most brothers don't get those two weren't, you know, screwing like a properly married duo—loopy for a man like *that*. (I should totally talk.) I mean, you don't force a tongue that long into celibacy— saw him do a Gene Simmons jamming at The Cheese...*ooo-baby*! But sweetie, you crank your hot water faucet off-on-off-on. Let's take a peeksy at your thingy with Sebastian—can I speak freely? You know I'm your *friend*. Sure, he's flaky as a box of grandma-washsoap. But when you two were singing lovey-dovey at the café I heard you hooked up with some chick? Then Rupi's bitching about you cutting his irises for a forgive-me-Sebastian bouquet? Then see-saw, you're off with Wiktor. And Józef. In Poland. How do we spell *glutton*?

Come home licking all the boy crumbs off your fingers. This isn't an intervention, I mean we're free here. Fully liberated! So how did Chris snag this ring anyway? I hear what's-her-name took everything except his guitars to New York. Brothers are *talking* honey, talky-talky-talky, and it's not very holy or bright.

Gloee

She chittered around the ashram
squirreled in light, ribby as a ballerina,
flitting backwards through doorways,

always backwards. Hair bobbing like a frayed tutu,
grey roots glinting beneath the blonde.
Clicking the tip of her tongue at her teeth
as if calling an invisible dog. Her boy-lover

wandering in with his wonky star-struck grin—
thirty years and a hundred volts between them.
Even if you couldn't see auras you'd get the sense

she glowed. She could snap another brother inside out
with a brush of her shoulder, arc spasms of energy
through an unwitting body—have you starfished
on the dining hall floor, psychotropic, gone.

She was the real deal—some kind of lightening rod.
So much light she seemed out of control.
And didn't everyone want it.

*

I was assigned Barn duty: a bee-hive of haunted
rooms in the furnace-piped underbelly of the dorms.

Devotees dropping their junk into sorting bins,
and there on the schedule, Gloee, penned

next to mine. She'd tip-toe in, angel-marionette,
find my mind in a moment
and scoop me out of my head. She'd lift me

from my worries and fears, float me to the ceiling
and keep me there, hanging
like my own halo, seeing everything
through a golden lens. With Gloee

an hour of service flowed like effortless
minutes, sorting clothes onto hangers,
shelving LP's, penny dreadfuls, bric-a-brac.
When we'd emptied the day's donations

she'd whisper *thank you*. I'd nod and smile
high as a flag pole, always amazed
she could speak. Then she'd kite away backwards,

and my mind would tumble in, tears rolling
with the shock of re-entry.

*

When we could count ribs through her sweater,
when her breath soured and veins corded
the backs of her hands, the brothers mostly

abandoned her. Her lover
left for the ashram in Germany. They all
rolled their eyes, avoided her

jerky sparrow steps. *You're not a body, Gloee,*
they'd say. *Change your mind, heal yourself.*

Some days I teaspooned tiny portions
of supper onto her saucer. She'd whisper
That's enough and hunch at a far table

by the broken bain-marie. *You must eat
more,* they'd say. *You're not just light, Gloee.*

*

There was no service, no wake. Nothing
to mark her passing—I don't know who
emptied her room, slid her slippers from the foyer.

She left me her boxy beater sedan,
puckered with dents, trunk brimming
with Barn junk—pulp romances, teen-sized

dresses, and an empty jewellery box
with a broken lid and wind-up key.
Although I took it with me, I don't recall
winding the box. It's sold now,

for a Loonie at a yard sale,
and I don't know what music it played.

Cult Life

i. The Master never reached to grope a breast or fondle my crotch during meditation. Didn't clout me on the side of the head, whack me in the third-eye, or ask if I had an inheritance to tithe. He never called me dummy, asshole, or Dead One in front of three-hundred brothers. And He didn't drag me through the crowd by the roots of my hair before morning Satsang.

ii. Memory's like a film you saw drunk, scenes out of order, everyone talking under water. Once I was the passenger in a Kombi dare-deviling the hairpin corners of Sydney's beach roads, the driver chasing a two-door who'd cut him off, the raddled van lilting at the bends, almost lifting a wheel. And I'm bracing myself against the dashboard, the ceiling, begging him to pull over. But the way I remember it now, I'm on the right-hand side of the van— passenger side in North America. Except that's the driver's side in Australia. My mind's done a switcheroo. Memory's like trying to carry a spider on a piece of paper out into the sunlight—it keeps dropping off the edge, and when you scoop it up again, a few legs stick out in a wonky way.

iii. People who left were good as dead. No threat of violence, but the darkness is doubly dark if you're handed illumination and then reject it. And the drop-outs slouched so grey and papery, oh-so-droopy and unwashed. As if they had a storm cloud of an aura, as if they were a contagion—so when you saw them, say at Wal-Mart, or the water park, you walked on by. You kept your light intact.

iv. Occasionally He'd show up at AA meetings—some of the brothers ran a prison ministry, so the twelve steps became part of our *awakening process.* I sometimes sat in, naming myself an alcoholic, meaning I was addicted to the suffering of human existence, coveting something concrete I could recover from. Claiming to belong to that clan of hard-core ex-addicts, each with a sponsor and a real disease. He'd introduce Himself as a recovered alcoholic. I hadn't yet heard the rumours—His protégé cleaned His room, always by herself, because of the bottles.

v. We had a cameraman who filmed hundreds of videos of The Master to send into the world, tilting the reflectors so His blue eyes lasered: it's all a dream and we need the light of His mind to wake up, He'd say, then we can all flash out together. Except it sounded way more complicated, sounded like He was onto something. And later, we would sit with Him, watching Him watch Himself for hours.

vi. I never thought of the ones who left until I left. We were told their grievances had grown wild, that they spent their time spinning tales about the ashram. But I waited endless tables at that restaurant, surrendering my tips to the cashier, scrubbing bathrooms with my toddler in tow, ironing uniforms in the airless summer swelter, those poodle skirts and blouses we donned as servers in that fifties-themed time-warp of a place. Earning three bucks an hour and handing over half my wage as my monthly tithe. Opening those lace curtains at nine AM, greeting the morning glories I'd helped plant in window boxes. Hipping to and fro across the chequered floor, spotting the occasional orb weaver stretching its web between climbing flowers. Its nibbed legs tugging each thread taut.

Ones Who Leave

We're speeding down I-90 toward the ashram,
easing in and out of silence, Americanos
between us in the drink holders, and a sweet
slab of rocky road. Thrift stores, cafés, second-hand
book shops in Chicago closing their day behind us.

Hilly farmland rolls beneath the overpass and away
like painted scenery for a model train.
Power lines toothpick into the distance, miniature
cattle, grain silos. We enter a stretch of cornfields

crepe-papering the landscape. The sky
won't shake off its blue. And we remember
what He said in Satsang, how the ones who leave won't
be able to return—they'll steer onto the parkway

and the ashram will blink out, everyone with it.
Only dead cornfields, He said, parched, unharvested,
stalks helter-skelter. We keep driving
through a great underworld of cornfields, epic
and ghostly and still. A sick feeling

in our guts, and it's not the rocky road. Could be
our conversation—does He know what
we're contemplating? The road's been veering
left for miles and we worry we've made

a wrong turn, looping back on ourselves,
never getting closer. We feel the ashram
dissolving, as if a slipstream
buoys the last whiff of laughter, the golden

peal of ascension shimmering above the fields.
The horizon haunts like The Master's eyes,
that lazuline blue settling upon itself
as if a veil has just been lowered.

Am the lyrics of your love ditty

granting of a penny wish
     druthers
something beloved
     Am truly all
those hackneyed phrases
shopworn and cloying
unbelieving

     Am madly
tripping light-headed
     fantastically
         smouldering the grass
with each step bursting
all the roses golden
     gilded
        everything I touch

Heart Sutra
gate gate pāragate pārasamgate bodhi svāhā

My child plucks petals in the Secret Garden Café on the eve of my wedding,
fills her plastic beaded handbag, the one my father bought her—both my parents

at the ashram! My fiancé's mother from Regina, his Harvard-genius brother.
The awkward conjunction of genetics and a desire to transcend the world.

The musicians hover between science and art, tuning their instruments
by ear, by heart. They can measure its frequency now, the heart—

not its rhythm, but a finer resonance, something electromagnetic—
the slow hail of a rose swelling. My bridesmaid hunches in giggling fits

when she's nervous. My daughter fidgets the silk flowers on her shoes,
my father tugs his French cuffs as we head towards my groom. The garden blooms

with devotees flying in and out of standing meditation
under fading September skies—gone, completely gone. The Guru hasn't shown—

He's beyond the world, in some sort of altered state
by sundown. Fairy globes sparkle on the deck, illuminate

glittery paper hearts pinned to the backs of chairs, railings, tree trunks. Love notes
shining on table legs, swinging from thorns on the primrose vine. Hail the *seva* of sweetness

on the buffet table, devotional offerings: rosewater lassi, toffeed profiterole tower,
passionfruit pavlova, marshmallowy *ptasie mleczko*—the enlightenment of sugar

waiting beyond the ceremony, on the other shore. Our best man sobs,
clutches the podium as he reads, his comb-over

lifting in the breeze. Our vows hail the elusive sound
of the heart—in Sanskrit *anahata* means unstruck,

unharmed. They say a roomful of people in heart mediation creates a silent
field others might fall into. My daughter scatters petals on our feet—my love

sinks to one knee, asks my child to be his child. If we could
peel away the façade of the world, all we'd see is light.

Presenting our Wedding Album to The Master

His room spins like a party wailing
across the midnight hour, all his noise-makers
giggle-weeping, besottedly flailing.
I used to be one of them. We wait in the doorway.
Cliff passes our album forward—the heft of a body
ferried over heads at a concert towards the stage.
The Master slaps it down on His mahogany table
next to a tin of salt water taffy. Everyone waits
to hear what He'll say.

*The last wedding was Marty and Shio's—everything later
is a replication.* Half the room ignites in exaltation.
He's revealed the meaning of life. Again.
Marty and Shio married years ago,
but our wedding was the day before yesterday—
if He'd opened the album He'd have seen us
lit from within. He'd have seen how beautiful I was.
He might have said our names in Satsang.
We might have stayed.

Dear One

: C'mon, up you get. Get outta that chair and dance! Ditch those wheels, you dummy—what you waiting for? You think you're that body? You think those are legs, think you're sick? You're not sick, you're a piece a shit.

: There she is, risen from the dead! Went to the dream hospital, had her dream diabetes dealt with. We're dreaming, people. She's not a body, look at that light! Isn't she beautiful? Here, pass this to Dottie-Anne. No, that way, pass it back. Have a good swig of that Cola. There's your medicine!

: You think you got cancer or something? Don't gimme a story. Go on clutch 'em tight. You think your story's true? Think I'm gonna heal you? Heal yourself! You've gotta give me your mind if you want me to heal it. You need a *little willingness*. Look at that sour puss. Oh boy, she's gonna bawl. Ah, forget it.

: How're you feeling this morning, Mimi? Huh? Don't close your eyes and get all transcendental, look at me! You expect Athena to wash your hair forever? Lift your arms up, lift 'em up! What's the matter, think that's a real body? Think they're real arms? It's a damn dream! Bah, you're all used up. Go on, get outta here. Get! I mean it. Get the hell out!

Departures

Midday under canopies, the lake
shrugs off its birch-mottled shadows,
holds the sky. Buddha pool, scrying bowl,

if you bend your ear, you might hear
what it is to be whole. *The answer
is always held*, He said, *within the question—*

. you suspect someone else said that first.
Sedges rub creased palms together,
pin-legged pond-skaters do their Jesus trick.

Water slurps the muddy shore,
constant as the sensation of breath observed
on your upper lip. Thoughts dragonfly

the inlet of awareness, quiver
the silvered mica of a wing. You flit after,
as if they'll feather an answer. He said:

*if you wanted one it'd already be yours—
let go of identity, remember
you've always been awake.* Lake exhales

against the rock. *These teachings
are millennia old.* These boulders
look as if they'll shoulder the water forever.

But soon the dam will break,
the lake will flee. A few years from now,
He will die. Bridges will crumble,

houses will slide into hightailing water.
You'll see it on YouTube—the whole lake will birl
away in one foaming moment.

After making found poems from His words

you find yourself using what He taught—how to catch
slippery thoughts, the slick ones flashing past like bronze
scale under pondweed. Is He speaking to you when He writes
You'll never be satisfied being a poet. He's dead.
You don't recall reading that. Is it meant for you now? Dead,
for Chrissakes. Dead. *All mind is eternal.* His words
are like carpenter ants tunnelling your drift wood brain—
people never get rid of ants. You flip through His book,
scanning for phrases beginning *I am,* stealing
what follows for a poem, but His words suck you in
like a kiss: *Haven't you ever been so in love*
you couldn't stand it? Just wanted to savour this incredible ecstatic

*annihilation...*You stop yourself
quoting the next half-page on love. He was a magician
tugging scarves from his fist. *Time is a sleight of hand.*
Knots blur into a single cloth. *Mind is sui generis.* The cloth flies
out of His ear. He's pouring milk into a newspaper funnel.
Any reasonable mind can see the absurdity
of physical reality. A milky dove swoops into the rafters.
He's about to saw a woman in half.
He's about to make you disappear.

Seven Reasons Why I'd Never Return

1. Jilly helps me plan my move to the main ashram, offers her palms flat like scales: "In this hand the beloved cat, in that hand enlightenment." One hand sinks on "cat," the other rises on "enlightenment." Cat. Enlightenment. Cat. Enlightenment.

2. We arrive in the apple blossom of spring, front stairs confettied with petals, five months later, winterstripped of sweetness, trapped in the rusty warmth of our room, unwilling to steer ice rink roads. Waiting for something downy to appear in The Barn.

3. No one knew what was happening—the energy, I mean—not The Master, not Athena, not even Delphyne, who taught me to inhale from corona to soles, slammed to my knees by the radiant payload of light. Retching against breakfast, maybe blacking out in the bathroom. For days shaking like a disaster victim, waking in livid sweats, dreaming a hot iron swiped down my back, dreaming I'm a bird with its wings ripped off.

4. Try being vegan in a cheese-lovin' region. From local haunts to the ashram dining hall the rising ripeness of cheese. Jack cheese salad, beer cheese soup, blue cheese dressing, fried cheese, cheese fries, cheese pie, cheese dumplings, cheesy doughnuts, cheesy pancakes, cheesy grins.

5. Black is soothing, sensual, is cosmic vastness. Let's be honest, it's slimming. The holy high-and-brights flittered the halls in whites, creams, baby pales—no one donned darkness, not after

copping a scorning as a newbie for your aura matching your black crotchet twinset.

6.   The temptation to return remained for years, eventually dwindled to infrequent plagues of wistfulness. What can I say about the haven of community? About breathing the same language, the same cosmology, the same daily purpose? What can I say about the safety of choicelessness? Thank god it's gone.

7.   Small towns are *o-so-small*. Ashrams, smaller still. It's simpler to live in a place where the only person I've slept with is my husband.

What She Remembers for Certain

She threaded a mobile,
a binding of herself to him,
stemming rows of beads along her quilt,
window's screened haze doubling
the chains, her fingers wiring
silver and shadow,
blown glass drops
of honey from her veins.

Her father said *he's a man* and this
felt an important distinction.
So she threaded that too—
one thousand flowers of millefiori beads,
the magic eye of a *dzi*.

He trucked back from New York,
a mango and a wilting bouquet,
her mixtape looping hope.
Divorce sealed and bloody.
That's the whole blooming truth.

Snapshot of his return: cinematic
trail of tea lights leading to the tub, no
she only played that scene over and over
in her head. Undressed,
veiled behind gauze drapes—
that's an earlier draft. In the end

she paced the room, clothed and ordinary,
anxious when he was late.

Her father journalled *He has forever
in his eyes.* So she held that
truth to the mirror
then knotted it—
Russian trade beads plunging
deep as an indigo vat.

He wrote her sweet guitar
lying on their bed, crooned
into the swaying mobile.
Taught her daughter to play
music, to fry eggs. Found her a tiny
guitar, called her his own.

Eventually he'd seal a ring
into a box of seashell pralines.
He'd beg a guy in a vinyl store
to shrink-wrap the chocolates,
ring within twinkling zircon
light she'd toe in the clover
outside their apartment. She'd lie
to the jeweller—the stone
was once her aunt's—
she lied a lot back then.

She strings a story
book self, with each pass
through memory's peephole—

photograph, journal entry,
someone else's anecdote. She alters
the arrangement, re-threads
the truth. Like a glass mobile,
it's constellating now.

Cult Life II

i. The day after they aired "Ashram or Cult" on the local network, The Master drove down to the five-and-dime Himself, bought a crate of grape Kool-Aid. They served it in the dining hall to whoops of laughter and glee. We did have a couple of suicides, a few ended up in psych wards. There was that twenty-something German guy who went catatonic. But they all missed the teaching—they didn't get it.

ii. How do people end up in a New Religious Movement? Jungians would probably see it, collective consciousness and all. Minds are joined. People get excited, zealous, think Beatlemania, think women racing the streets burning bras, Canadian hockey riots. But it's more than that, it's organized ecstasy—a rave DJ working the crowd into frenzy, the revival hall with full gospel choir and folks dropping in the aisles. It's a mass UFO sighting over Mexico City— suddenly everyone thinks they know what's going on.

iii. People who died were scorned for leaving their bodies behind—they weren't fully devoted. The whole teaching is you disappear from the world entirely, those who aren't with us are dead. The whole teaching is you're not a body. There is no world.

iv. You can fall in fondness with anyone when you're in the ditch together—it's that trench sense of camaraderie, it's reflexive oneness, it's what necessitates prayer. Unless someone's deeply done you in, it's unnatural to lose the love. Imagine trying to leave a few hundred people you've found a soft spot for.

v. The Master's daughter tells a childhood story: sometimes when they had dinner guests, her dad would place his plate on the floor after the meal, let the dog lick it clean. Then he'd casually slide it into the crockery cupboard. It was a family in-joke. It was a riot. There's a lot of power in knowing what others don't know. It's the principle of teaching.

vi. Humans have a proclivity for devotion. If not the spiritual Passion, then a lover, an art practice, a sports star. The Hindus have it easy: 33 million gods, best flavour for any *bhakti*. In the end it doesn't matter what we yield to—pray at the knees of a mountain; pour milk and ghee on a Shiva lingam stone. When the heart cave cleaves, it's there, the whole gyrating universe, wildly honed.

The Unnoticed

The one you are looking for is the one who is looking.
—St Francis of Assisi

We sing down the heavens
into the body of a lover.

The sky splits wide
and the scriptures are inked.

We waste at the feet
of the masters of plenty.

The rivers are forked
with trojan prayers.

We gambol the side streets
oiled with distraction.

A chrysalis pearl
in the hutch of the heart.

We wake from a nightmare
to find we're still dreaming.

Mountains vanish,
then reappear.

The Second You

For a long time your mind echoed
like black keys on a piano. *Who am I?*
Who am I? you'd ask yourself, crawling
through hollow logs in your dreams,
the kelpy tang of a strange shore,
water rising around you.

*

On the night of your wedding,
a shooting star. First ever and heading northwest.
Friends paid for a hotel overlooking a lake,
the whole place oddly empty. You swooshed
the halls, veil kiting, expecting
other guests, hoping to show off
your new husband, your billowing dress,
but you only encountered that star.

*

In your twenties, you'd visited two palmists
and neither could reveal why halfway around
your plush mount of Venus, the lifeline
ended abruptly and began again upward
and to the left. One guessed
illness, career change. The other drew Death
from the deck. *But everyone knows*

that's transformation, she said, and quickly
flipped another card.

*

They told you the darkness would be doubly
dark. They said you'd be left behind, here
another thousand years, you'd miss out
on your own enlightenment. They said
it doesn't matter what you say
it's all pearls and swine
out there, no one will ever hear you.

*

Leaving was an act of abscission. You sloughed
your Selkie pelt, and there you were,
an unexceptional woman
in jeans, on a stony beach, on a West Coast island,
an ex-devotee husband and a six-year-old.
Bleached logs laddering a stony shore,
flat grey ocean lipping another dialect.
Maple leaves, a bouquet of fluxy yellows
starred in your child's fist.

Acknowledgements

With gratitude to the following literary journals and anthologies who published earlier versions of poems in *Cult Life*: *Best Canadian Poetry*, *The Fiddlehead*, *The Rusty Toque*; *PRISM International*, *Room Magazine*; *Arc Poetry Magazine*, *The Antigonish Review*, *The Literary Review of Canada*, and *Plentitude Magazine*.

Thank you to the Canada Council for the Arts for the gift of time—that first year of unhindered writing was vital.

Thank you to the talented team at Pedlar Press for making me feel at home and offering such excellent support in all areas: Beth Follett for reaching into her many hats and pulling out a wonderland of readings, Emma Allain for beautifully rendered design (and those never-ending galleys), and to my extraordinary and meticulous editor, Monica Kidd.

Many thanks for permission to use of the lines of poetry that begin each section:

Part I: from *Quick* by Anne Simpson. Toronto: McClelland & Stewart, 2007. Part II: lines from Ghalib translated by Adrienne Rich reprinted with permission from *The Hudson Review*, Vol. IV, No. 4 (Winter 1969–1970). Copyright © 1970 by The Hudson Review, Inc.
Part III: lines from *At the Edge of the Chopping there are No Secrets* reprinted with permission from the estate of John Thompson.

Immense thank yous to the following professorial mentors for inspiring me and raising me as a writer with expertise, rigor and hugely generous hearts (in alphabetical order): Lorna Crozier, Carla Funk, Bill Gaston,

John Gould, Lorna Jackson, Joan MacLeod, Tim Lilburn and Steven Price. And to John Barton for his friendship and faith, and for countless and invaluable hours of poetry exchange. Thank you also to my various poetry cohorts and writerly friends for camaraderie, inspiration and suggestions par excellence. I must also thank Anita Lahey, for her life-changing recommendation, and Valerie Tenning, without whom my university years would have been vastly more difficult.

With deep bows and gratitude to the many "ashram" people (friends and fellow artists, ardent spiritual seekers)—you made it possible for me to tell this tale by bravely living your own truth. Like me, you sought an experience beyond the ordinary, and I wish each one of you all goodness—if it doesn't seem so in this book, it's because emotional truth and narrative arc must sometimes trump factual truth when crafting life stories into (what one hopes might be) literature.

To my father for the first gift of real poetry—Neruda's *Yellow Heart*, and to my mother and so many family members for hearty encouragement and support.

And finally to my husband, my love, my best friend, my first reader... Chris, thank you for more than I can ever list, and thank you for naming this book. To my oldest child, my beautiful one, who lived this with me. And to my sweetest Sonnet, who kept me grounded through the edits.

Notes

The Master poems are constructed from the text *Discourses from The Master*, a collection of talks recorded and transcribed by devotees and bound at the ashram press. "Who is The Master" uses only intact sentences, while the others use phrases or fragments—words are often extracted, but no words are added.

In *Heart Sutra*, the words from the Buddhist mantra of the same name are woven throughout the poem. A common translation of the mantra is: "Gone, gone, gone completely, gone completely beyond, Enlightenment hail!"

The word "winterstripped" in "Seven Reasons Why I'd Never Return" is admiringly borrowed from Lucia Perillo's poem, "Say This."

Some names used in the book are names given by The Master (or in some cases by previous gurus), others have been invented to represent composite characters. The names listed in "The Master Attempts to Christen Me" are all names he bestowed. Unless permission has been given, all real/current names have been changed out of respect for privacy.

Kyeren Regehr holds an MFA in Creative Writing from the University of Victoria and was awarded the Victoria Medal for Fine Arts upon completion of her undergraduate degree. She enjoyed several years on the poetry board of *The Malahat Review*, and has twice received grants from the Canada Council for the Arts. Her work has been published in literary journals and anthologies in Canada, the United States, and Australia. Kyeren lives on Vancouver Island, B.C.